Sidewalk Drafts

Typewriter Poetry
in Passing

Sidewalk Drafts
Typewriter Poetry in Passing

A.D. Bullock

Copyright 2025 by ADBullock

All rights reserved. This book or any portion thereof may not be reproduced or used in any manner whatsoever without the express written permission of the publisher except for the use of brief quotations in a book review.

ADBullock

adbpoetry@gmail.com

Print ISBN: 979-8-218-69910-9

For Charlotte,

without whom these poems would surely not exist

On 3.5"x5" slips of paper, these poems were written in public on a 1963 Smith Corona Sterling typewriter between 2022 and 2025 at a number of different locations in and around Denver, Colorado. In preparation for this compilation, each poem was edited for typos (there were many) and grammar.

These poems were written in ten to twenty minutes each. To retain their original imperfections and to honor the spirit of the exercise, any additional edits to a poem were limited to changes of enjambment, punctuation, and the occasional word alteration. The typewriter can switch to red ink which is, unfortunately, not reflected here. These pages maintain a high fidelity to the original works. The font selected here, Prestige Elite, is of the same family as the typefont on the typewriter and appears very similar.

Many of these poems are posted to the Instagram account adb_poetry. On that platform, they are expanded and edited with alternative endings.

Preface

What poem does the world need right now? What poem do you need - just for you? And what if you could, simply by asking, bring that poem to life - no matter the topic, event, or subject?

This book genuinely wants to know because this book is about the poetry people carry around inside themselves all day, everyday, but do not talk about.

****

Every Sunday, from May to November, dozens and dozens of stalls line South Pearl Street in Denver, Colorado for the weekly farmer's market. Amidst the smells and music, each tent offers something delicious, unique, fresh or beautiful. The many vendors with their work up for display, seem animated and excited to share this piece of their life with others. Without fail, each tent sports a big sign explaining what they offer to draw people in.

Propped up in the shade of two Honey Locust trees is something different: a little table, a little chair, and a little paper sign.

The typewriter certainly turns heads. In fact, it's the noise; there's something about the click-clack of the keys that seems to slow people down long enough for their curiosity to get the better of them.

Taped to the table, the paper sign is in marker: Give a prompt. Get a poem. Donate if it feels good.

People stare, smile, move on. Some linger, think, chat. Others know immediately what they need and simply place their order. But inevitably, the prompts come in:

Bumblebees in Love
Fate
Cheese
Letting Go
A Frog Eating Ice Cream
Life in Your Twenties
A Tortoise Shell Cat Named: Rude
Nature ? Spring

The moment someone commits to their prompt may be the most exciting part of the whole process. Prompts come from groups, from individuals, from kids and grandparents. They come from happy people, lost people, grieving people - people who seem surprised they're asking for a poem at all. They give prompts about the future, about the past, about someone far away. Prompts about dragons and flowers and God and healing.

Quite often, people ask 'how it works.' So far, only four rules have become necessary:

One, you must provide the prompt.

Two, a love poem for someone else will not be written. You should write it!

Three, it's good that people love their dog. Everyone loves their dog. Too many people want poems of their dog. If you want a poem about your dog, pricing is inflated and subject to change. How cute your dog is will not change this.

Four, AI is never involved.

Eventually, they select their prompt, a delivery time is set, and they walk away. Then more typing.

Typically, their prompt becomes their title, and each prompt gets ten to fifteen minutes of writing - depending on how chatty the market is that day. Eventually, the 'promptee' returns and then they listen to their poem. Which is the second most exciting part.

****

It's a strange phenomenon to be confronted with the request for a prompt - a mirror asking you to identify something with poetic potential. Something you want to understand differently or deeper. Something you believe deserves greater attention. It's just a normal Sunday morning and most people don't have a topic immediately. But some people do. In fact, some of the best are when people arrive in a huff as if they have a script from their doctor and are late to run more errands. At first, the purely transactional quality of the interaction could be off putting. But when they hear the poem out loud, it often resonates with more clarity because the poem addresses something important they've been carrying around, but have yet to name or untangle. Often, we talk for a while and they explain, directly or indirectly, why this is their prompt. Regardless, everyone comes needing something.

After hundreds of prompts, the trends for personalized poetry revealed some lovely things about humans. We are creative and silly; we're curious and reverent; we're sympathetic and very capable of surprising ourselves. And from all these interactions, two things became clear.

First, most prompts beget poems that loosely fall into one of four groups or genres. I once described these genres based on what the prompt asks the poet to be: sometimes the poem asks for a therapist; other times a priest; sometimes a fortune teller; sometimes a philosopher. But a more accurate study of the prompts makes clear that it's, of course, not about the poet at all; it's about what kind of meaning making the promptee hungers for. Here, they're grouped into Joy, Gratitude, Conviction, and Hope.

The second thing all these interactions revealed is how we are starved for a certain kind of meaning. Not to say we don't have meaning in our lives, we certainly do; friends, family, pets, careers, spirituality, hobbies, projects, even small quiet moments of the day can build meaning. Rather, we are starved for a particular kind of meaning: meaning in the form of a gift. Not some load-bearing aspect of our life that we construct intentionally, but something serendipitous. A silent meaning that springs from inside us and is reflected by a poem.

For example, of the people who hear their poem and cry, appear shocked, or give profuse thanks, I don't believe the reaction is due to the quality of the poem. I believe it's from the gratitude of seeing something special - something superfluous - materialize just for them. For that reason, "Donate if it feels good" is very intentional phrasing. Ideally, people feel they are not simply paying for a poem, but donating as recognition that the process and effect of poetry in this raw, live, typewriter format is worthwhile.

Perhaps it's not surprising, but it was a prompt that helped form this theory. In our brief chat, a pair relayed how they had a top-hat-wearing uncle who also wrote for people on a typewriter and they wanted to send him a poem ...

Uncle Jim - A Typewriter Poet

8.13.2023
~ Eric

Hello from afar,
my tall-hatted friend.
These people tell me
you have a beautiful heart,
that it beats so loud
the seams split
and so full, you cannot help
but let your art flow from
the rips.

They say you might like to hear from a peer -
someone else who likes
the rush of the crowd
and the small orbits
we produce.
Brief moments that let a stranger
open a drawer of their mind
and share it in the light.
Someone who honors
the privilege of holding their dreams,
prompts, and fears
and telling them:
       "This is good.
       You have poetry in you."

This collection celebrates the moments when complete strangers were vulnerable enough to 'open the drawer of their minds' in broad daylight. These poems were selected because they represent, not only those strangers' bravery, but consequently, the poetry they accessed within themselves. Innate within us all, we harbor something that is worthy of care, respect, and meaning. When we share it, in the light, we are more human, more connected, and more alive.

So, what is your prompt?

Contents

Preface

Chapter One: Joy

1   Rainbows
2   Foster Parents
3   Going to College
4   End of the School Year
5   Graduate
6   Letting Go
7   Perspective
8   New Beginnings: Moved in Together
9   Invisible String Theory
10   Marrying Your Best Friend
11   Bumblebees in Love
12   Panda & Turtle
13   Angry Weiner Dog
14   The Joys of Simple Pleasures
15   Contentment vs Growth

Chapter Two: Gratitude

18   Snap Peas
19   Nature ? Spring
20   Sweetness. Love. Sunday
21   A Dog Named Bean
22   Awe & Wonder: The Freshness of The Breeze & The Birds
23   Independence in Summer
24   Summer Vacation Home
25   Crying on Your Birthday
26   Life in Your Twenties
27   How to Discover Your Inner Genius
28   New Beginnings: Moving in Together
29   Life's Good - Maybe a Baby
30   Our Daughter
31   Empty Nesting
32   Mother in Switzerland

Contents

33   Long Distance Best Friends
34   Sisters
35   Grief
36   Motorcycle Adventure
37   My Dog, My Human

Chapter Three: Conviction
40   Anarchist Orca Whales
41   Lost in Space: Final Thoughts
42   Fire is a Purifier
43   Fly Fishing
44   What is the Definition of Happiness
45   What To Do With Ones Life
46   Self Love
47   Fate's Arrival
48   Rejection
49   Love
50   Love
51   Baby Daddy aka Cheating Ass
52   Healing
53   New Beginnings

Chapter Four: Hope
56   Change
57   New Beginnings
58   Welcome to Your Twenties
59   Sunday at the Farmers Market
60   Embarking on a New Chapter
61   Nervous to Talk to New People
62   First Love
63   Heartbreak
64   Phoenix
65   Water
66   Mushrooms & Seasonal Depressnnnnnnnn
67   Saturn 29
68   Florida.Hot.Queer.Welcome
69   Love

Contents

- 70   Cheese
- 71   To Coach
- 72   Summer to Fall
- 73   Resiliency
- 74   A Tortoise Shell Cat Named: Rude
- 75   A Squid Who is in Love with the Sun

Chapter One

Joy

Rainbows

5.5.2024

~ Jill

Of course the colors.
Let's just get that out of the way.
But it wasn't the colors that made
you sit, made you relish the rain
       soaking up your jeans.
       It was something about the silence
       of the massive architecture floating
       in its own diaphanous
       impossibility.
No opening score, no fanfare.
No reporters or Instagram shutters framing
their glamorous muses.

A stillness that almost
eclipses the storm - a silence
that at least puts the thunder
in doubt.
Doubt that grafts a hope -
that scrubs the fear out
of your ears until
only a heartbeat remains in the quiet.
Until the gloom is scoured away to just
a bright stain for the prism of us to wonder at
until the birds begin to stir again.

Foster Parents

7.14.2024

~ Alex

There has been an extra room
of my heart for years.
I tried it as an office
       a studio messy with
       the paints.
I tried it as a guest room
       and the one cold winter
       where I closed it off completely
       and cut the heat.

Butterflies find their way in.
Pollen from the stars
       light the corners.
       I cannot keep life out.
       Though I check the locks
       and chock the shutters.
The ladybugs slide on in
       and vines rush up
       over the sill.
I cannot help it.

You helped me sweep it out,
clean it up, usher out the
bugs and buds and heat.

But today is too much
and must be shared - everyone
must have a place & I must
offer mine.

Mine where the
stars cannot be deterred.

Going to College

7.30.2023

~ Bridgette

There will be many late nights.
Few, but some, sunrises.

You will learn facts
and plenty of concepts.

You will master the art
of procrastination.

You will never learn how to cite.
And nearly all of this vast
and rich vein of time
plunging through your new chapter
will one day be void.
Save for an armful of the most
precious memories. Don't worry,
just those few will be plenty.
But they will not be the ones
you expect.

We think it is an adventure
when look ahead and cannot
clearly see.
We know it was an adventure when
we look back and cherish the mundane:
late nights with a friend we never
could have imagined.
A friend we couldn't now imagine life without.
Maybe with a coffee. A story.
And them teaching you something -
how to cite your paper perhaps.

End of the School Year

6.9.2024
~ Adrien

Papers and equations,
deadlines, late nights,
the cramming and the lectures,
and the cramming and the grades,
      and the cramming and more cramming.

My brain is saturated
      and I refuse to learn
      or be taught or listen.

School is out which means
I can finally catch up
with the deferred growth
of my heart and my life -
can finally meditate
on this newest chapter of freedom
and who I believe I must be.

School does not teach us
      how to apologize well,
      how to forgive with grace,
      how to take our overflowing head and pour
          it onto the seeds
          we love, we need, we fear.

Summer is for tardiness,
for running with scissors,
for burning our notes -
dancing around the heat.

Graduate

8.6.2023

~ to my sister

They have taught your hands
      to draw and mend,
      to work a needle and a blade.
They taught you metrics
      and equations,
      how to read the posture of health
      in both number and pulse.
They introduced you
      to the combat
      of virus and dose,
      of inoculation and breath.

But they could not prepare your heart
for this grand authority.
The words, wings, and many classrooms
could never clothe you for the weather
in our chests.
The doctors and PhD's won't dare attempt
to improve what could never be taught:

Your compassion and conviction
will not fit in the syringes,
they cannot be prescribed.
But they are your most valuable utensils.
They taught your hands many things,
but never doubted your heart.

Letting Go

7.23.2023
~ Jackie

We feel powerful
when we can keep things
in our orbit. Our many
satellites held tight in ellipse.
Our heavy gravity reaching
out further and further
into the chaotic void.
We 'feel' powerful
and may even enjoy the daily
organizing, labelling, and straightening
of all our hearts many anchors.

But all these swarming planets
push and pull our tides,
leave us constantly
too high, too low,
dry and disformed.
It is beautiful to release them -
to let our waters go still
and to watch the comets streak
across our empty skies.
We feel free when we clear ourselves
and what is power without freedom?

Perspective

6.25.2024

~ Anonymous

You don't know you are wrong yet.
Just as I don't know
you could be right.

But our volume says otherwise
and a race to the bottom takes two.

Surely if we hold tighter
to our hot utensils we can dismember
this fight into bite-sized pieces
and feast at far ends of the room.

But somehow, even in your wrongness,
you fill me.
So the plates grow cold
and we consider the Tupperware.
We consider ice cream.
Champagne - why not?
Chilled and served with no knives,
no flame.
Silence as we toast to our wrongness
and race to the bottom of the glass -
race to uncork another.

New Beginnings: Moved in Together

5.5.2024

~ Brittany

Today is not yesterday
      which I can no longer
      steer or dream of.
And today is not tomorrow
      which I cannot yet bare
      to cage in plans and designs.
Or at least,
no plans or designs
that don't have you.

Today there is a new ceiling above us,
      walls that we will make our own,
      will paint in many coats of memories:
      murals of morning sheets with you,
      still-lifes of you
      sleeping through the movie,
      impressions of our lucid dreams,
      portraits of us tomorrow
            laughing
                  at how much
                  we changed
                  overnight.

Laughing at all we didn't know
which is, I suppose,
the best beginning.

Invisible String Theory

6.9.2024

~Jazz

It was a strange sensation
to feel the knots
come undone.
       The occasional tug
       as you grew closer, pulled
       further.

Stranger still to feel
the unspooled fabric of my heart
       begin to reel itself together,
       to weave tight and tight
       and tighter.

It took me a while to realize
it wasn't a web I was in,
not a trap or snare.
It took some heartbreak and silly mistakes
to follow the pull - to trust it.

It was a strange sensation
as I wound the yarns around my hand,
following blindly
to finally find the end -
       a frayed cut
       and a waiting smile.
A strange sensation
to be both unbound & completely tied to you.

*The 'invisible string theory' is the concept
that a string connects you to your soul mate*

Marrying Your Best Friend

8.20.2023
~ Chris

These first five years
have been informative -
        I now know what that tone means,
        and all your favorite flavors;
        I know how to make you laugh,
        and when not to.

I know the dreams
you harbor - silent and waiting;
the ones you work like origami
but keep flat, not yet up & living.

I know your stories.
These first five years taught me many things:
how to be your witness & hold the loose ends
of your difficult days.
They taught me how I would not trade
our worst days
for anything: to see the fight set in your jaw,
and turn it - against the odds - into a smile,
a laugh, a victory for us.

These five years taught me
my best friend & I can conquer
the trials of love - the many demands
of Forever.

That we can fold each other flat
& breath in life each time.

Bumblebees in Love

5.5.2023

~ Bethany

There are many rooms, though small,
in the breezy expanse
of the high mountain fields.
Many rooms if one knows
where to look.

Within the tulip walls and rose curtains,
the mallow drapes and syringa fountains,
one may find the bumblebees
going about the quiet duties of love.

Having left the hive behind for now,
they stitch their looping orbits together
in ballooning courtship dances.
They tune their buzzing
to harmonize, they prepare the pollen
how the other likes,
they tell their stories
and listen as only a bee can listen:
    with a hundred eyes,
    the biggest love their small bodies can fit
    and the belief that everything they touch
    is sweet.

Panda & Turtle

8.18.2024
~ Andrea

One never intends to grow
the way the world has in mind,
or so it seems.
The shell was not my idea,
nor was the achingly slow cadence.

And you say your playful tumbles
were not the fierce
apex instincts you expected.

To be what the world made us is not so bad.
We are, after all, soft beings
who are looking for a home.
Dreams of flight or to be the impossible size
of the whales - those paths still call to me.
But we know.

How would I watch the world form around me?
      Or appreciate the calm
      as the others rush by?
How could you coax
      your giddy joy out of such monotony
      of bamboo repetition?

How many times have we wanted
what we do not like?
Covet what made us further from home?
I may still dream of wings,
but I'll adore all the gifts
the world has in mind
from the slow vantage of my shell.

Angry Weiner Dog

9.10.2023
~ Shelby

They say cats can have a mean-streak.
They haven't met me.
My righteous fury
is wolf-like, well before
domestication.
That legs this short
can carry rage this tall
is a testament to my pure breed
and the compulsion of my crusade.

Neither pacts nor treaties,
no resolution or white flag,
will save you.

This is dog-eat-dog ...
and speaking of eating -
isn't it about that time?

I wouldn't want a small
squabble to break tradition...
I think we can set aside our
differences, at least
for dinner.

And perhaps something from
the table? A morsel as token
of our forgotten disputes?
After all, only cats
keep their grudges.

The Joys of Simple Pleasures

8.2.2024

~ Amelia

We love the sweater for its tired hue,
      its forgotten
      tears and pulls.
We love wearing it when
      the leaves protest against
      the glass, when we hear
      the oven strain
      in the other room as it bends
      into the heat.
We love the book, closed in our
hands, with something to tell us, something
we could never expect.

They are small enough
      to neglect without punishment
      yet sustain us if we let   them -
      the loom of our hearts
      working thread after thread,
      into something big,
      something that cares
      for us, and keeps us warm.

We love the sweater for tonight,
      but also for each knot,
      for the patches, where it's
      been & who gifted it to us.
We love it because it smells
like stillness, like you in the
other room, like rips & tears
and mending. Like making joy
thread by thread.

Contentment vs Growth

6.18.2023

~ Tim

The shoots sing in a falsetto green, the alto
of the birds urging them on.
In a rare respite, the farmer watches. Hot gloves
in a pocket.

It is slow, hard work
to grow straight up,
but the shivs of green do not complain
of their silent struggle.

He wonders
how far they must feel
from the cool comfort of the seed,
the delicious sleep beneath the soil,
the contentment before birth.

He wonders
what if he had stopped?
The row half planted,
the invitation to life withheld.
What if he had slept in?
It is hard work to stand straight up,
harder still to bend over. But the green chorus
wakes him each morning,
content with their song.

One of the first poems written at the S. Pearl St. Farmer's Market, Tim is a local farmer who ran the stall adjacent

Chapter Two
Gratitude

Snap Peas

8.13.2023
~ Medha

I remember those bright
early days - some of my first -
when the neighbor's garden
would fascinate. When it would transform
from desiccated soil
to a green wonder.

I remember us sneaking away to count the buds
and smell the soil.
I remember the heat under
the great big leaves and it humming
down onto our young hands
as we picked tomatoes and pulled
the tender carrots.
But most of all, I remember
the sweet plump sabers
of the snap peas.
The snare of their vines
twisting into nowhere.

Those bright early days are gone
and the raised beds
are surely flat earth once again.
But yesterday can be forever
when handled correctly.
You must take the memory in your fingers,
twist as you pull,
and let the juice
run down your wrist.
The flavor will never grow old.

Nature ? Spring

5.5.2024

~ Camille

Spring is full of typos
and first drafts:
      the birds remembering
      slowly their songs,
      the blooms late and uneven,
      the many greens not yet finding
      their harmony as Monet would order them.

The frost demands a slew of revisions,
the redactions severe.
But it is an effective editor
and reminds us of the last, cold chapter -
the one we finished and finished again.

A swelling warmth animates the day in a way
the winter never could - pushing
the soil's dark scent into the streets,
splitting the colors across the sky,
plucking a chord in my chest
that I forgot I had,
a harmony the birds remember immediately.

Sweetness. Love. Sunday

8.10.2023
~ Josh

Sundays are for resting.
For quiet blasphemy.
For white painted rooms
and soft sunlight.
For too much coffee.
For too much cream.
Sunday is for slow and easy.
Slower than that.
Even slower.

Don't walk so fast, you'll miss
the cool hem of the shade.
Don't talk so fast,
you won't hear the love song
in my silence.

Slower.
There is more than caffeine
in these veins.
Listen to the heart beat,
there is a melody I can't control -
so easy and so innate
I can do nothing else.

Slower - so slow this poem
is our map for the whole day.
I don't want it to end -
refuse, in dusk light, to read
the final line.

A Dog Named Bean

7.23.2023
~ Andie

You will spend your forever with me
and I made that decision for you.

That you trust me both blindly
and with such unerring zeal,
bestows within me
one of my favorite joys
wrapped and ribboned in
endless layers of responsibility.

You rely on me
to work the impossible gate latches;
you trust me to navigate
these many teeming streets;
and you choose daily
to believe your devotion to me
is repaid in kind.

You will spend your forever
with me - trusting perfectly.
And I will spend forever
trying to earn it.

Awe & Wonder: The Freshness of The Breeze & The Birds
11.05.2023

~ Jackie

It is a privilege to be alive.
It's easy to forget this.
Too easy.
The way the soft grasses
hold the light, the fluid
dream of the clouds, even the timid smell
of the blanching roses
under their sheath of frost can be forgotten.
Can be missed.
Can be left behind in a childhood blanket
    that held
    tight your
    precious
    touchpoints of life.

You are invited to the grand
& the humble, the rare &
the pedestrian - all the
unnecessary that is this world.
You are invited to the Awe,
to the Wonder. To the freshness
of the breeze on your wrists,
and, of course, the birds.

Independence in Summer

5.19.2024

~ Sophia

My winter molt is finally off.
The spring cleaning is
..mostly.. done.

And now no one can tell me
      what to do. What to eat.
      How much to drink, or that hair of the dog
      is a bad decision.

No one will caution me the water's too cold,
      the summit's too far, or the stray cat
      could never love me back.

I will let the sun do what it wants with my hair,
      let the mornings gorge me
      with coffee, let the evenings
      convince me this freedom is nonrefundable.

This summer is for hot streets, an endless
breeze dripping green from the trees.
What is independence
without some decadence?
What is more decadent than summer?

Summer Vacation Home

10.1.2023
~ Eva

It's the smell.
More than anything - the wet cedar,
the wet grass, the wet sky
and all of it reaching into our hair,
our pockets, our loose memories
as they ruffle in the Denver wind.

It was always the magic of it that gripped us:
       transporting us not to a different place,
       but a whole separate arc of time,
       parallel and sweet.

In this arc
I get to keep you and me and us
as we were: indelicately comfortable
in the deep chairs - fully unspooled
with the soft hiccups of the lake
beneath us & beneath the boards.
I get to have you and me and us as we are -
the sole owners of our most precious memories,
exotic flotsam from a distant
country of the heart,
a different world. One we go to
whenever I smell wet cedar.

Crying on Your Birthday

7.9.2023

~ Savannah

This day is for you.
Congratulations, you have the immense privilege
      of breathing,
      of feeling,
      of walking the warm ground
      with those you love.

The Suggestion Box for Life
      has been full for millennia:
      more sleep,
      fix the whole 'heartbreak' thing,
      and hangovers have much room
      for improvement.
Our cosmic artists work out the bugs;
they do their best.

But this day is for you.
We are not here to celebrate the days.
We are here to honor what is yours:
      it may not be what you asked for,
      but these tears are yours -
      no one else's.
No one will feel it for you.
Cry all day! It is a worthy use of your time.
And, though we don't celebrate the days,
the next one may be better.

Life in Your Twenties

11.5.2023

~ *Lindsey*

It's nearly impossible to give advice.
      You will make mistakes.
      They will be marvelous,
      and silly, and often
      irreversible. They will make you better.
      They will be the stories
      of your life.

It's easier to give encouragement.
      Despite the recurring and conspicuous
      lack of clear direction, your heart
      is strong enough to be lost
      and enjoy it. Mostly.

And it is necessary to give a welcome:
      the rest of us greet you warmly.
      You are in the rush of life now.
      Really in it.
      Its confusion and its beauty.
      Its mystery and its naked vistas.
      The overwhelming volume and the delicate
      punctuations of silence.

Here is your invitation:
      Trust in yourself will not diminish
      your challenges,
      but it will make you free.

RSVP asap.

How to Discover Your Inner Genius

9.27.2023

~ Emery

The poets want so badly to drift
into the clean solitude of the mountains,
      the forests, the silence of the muse.

The artists with their brushes
let their feet pull them up the hungry staircases
      buoying them higher to see more,
      to see further - the colors intoxicating.

The philosophers slowly tumble
to the soft beaches to count the waves,
      to find the melody,
      not quite waiting, not quite solving.

We feel about in the dark of
our hearts for the flint
      to our steel.
Not that we will see,
but because we know warmth
even when we have never had it.

Beyond the fear of the fire, after the fun
of its shadows, we remain close
      to its sighs & sputters
      for our fascination.

What will you study like this -
what will you question
until it is only smoke?

New Beginnings: Moving in Together

6.9.2024

~ Sequoia

Funny how sometimes
a newness is simply a continuation:
      the two of us halting,
      agreeing 'This, yes, & more tomorrow.'
      The song ongoing
      but somehow changed.

We will have our walls
      & our mugs - our green leaves
      greeting us each morning.

We will have our walks
      & our fights and trips without
      risk of missing you.

We have had walls and coffee
& many meals,
but that was when
we were different,
      before the song
      scooped us up, had us lose our timing,
      find a new rhythm
      find new streets and art
      and the tantric mystery
          of enjoying you
          not as You, but 'We' -
relishing the fulcrum of before & after.

Life's Good - Maybe a Baby

8.2.2024

~ Jared

It is too easy for small moments
      to roll across
      the uneven floors of our days
      and be lost - their joys -
      in the dark corners.
It takes a moment of quiet
to hear them scrawling along
the baseboards - to recognize:
      Life is Good, we are good.
          Happy and healthy,
almost surprised
by our sidewalk audit as we catch
the others eyes and smile.

At home, the cat waits for us
to roll more memories across
the kitchen - to watch our recipes,
      to hear about the trails and peaks,
      and to cock her head
      when we begin listing names -
      ones she does not yet have
      a face for. Ones we laugh at,
      shake our heads,
          say No until we say Yes.

It is too easy to be dissatisfied.
Unless I am with you.
In Colorado. And maybe a baby.

Our Daughter

8.18.2024
~ Justin

Today is for slamming doors;
       you are getting quite good at it.

I wish you could have seen me
       at my prime - I could bust hinges
       and pop knobs with the best.

Today is for a healthy dose
of confusion.
When happiness from yesterday
       does not feel like happiness today.
       Anger, not like anger.
       And Help, not like help.

Though it may sound impossible,
we do understand.
We still read the language of silence,
are still fluent in sarcasm.
We remember the beautiful disaster that is today.

Today is for growth.
You are getting quite good at it.
Even with no map, no instruction.
We'll be waiting, when you open
the door, to hold you
as a child, as a girl, and a woman.
We are getting good at Today.

Empty Nesting

6.25.2023

~ Suzanne

Where have you been
amidst these many loud rooms?
Even in the conspicuous silence,
I could not find you.
But the stillness revealed
      both your trail and, finally,
      where you placed what we had set down
      all those years ago.

That instrument on which your young voice
shone so well. Those maps
we once knew by heart. The recipe
neither child liked
and so we have not tasted in decades.

I hear your approach
and look up from the dusty shelves,
the many open boxes, and the creased dreams.

You smile.
Where have you been, I ask.
No, you say, where shall we go?

Mother in Switzerland

7.14.2024
~ Gisela

They say time is the greatest distance
between two hearts. This watery barrier
lies between the You I've carried with me
the last two years
and the one I know
is walking cobbles
thousands of miles away,
laughing, holding friends,
and, I hope, drinking good wine.

The blessing to have you so close -
to have the You I've loved,
without the easy nourishment of seeing your eyes,
hearing the small, insignificant stories
that compose your day - that blessing
will return to me.
Return via those stories, those sweet crumbs
that lead by new paths
to the oldest shrine I have left to me:
any room where we are together.

Long Distance Best Friends

8.20.2023

~ Jordan

I can hear the smile in your voice -
      funny what parts of you
      can travel via phone line.
      Funny how much of you fits
      in the palm of my hand
      all the way from NYC:
I see your flashing eyes,
your hair I always loved,
and three books worth of our stories - redacted
for all but us two. Redacted heavily at parts.

You continue to ship pieces of us
across the miles.
The joke we won't let die,
the Starwars pun I should have seen coming,
the reassurance I didn't know I needed
that you gave so effortlessly.

Despite how much of you I get
from afar, there is no substitute
for my sister.
Funny how much of you I need
and how little of you can sustain me
2,000 miles away.

Sisters

8.2.2024

~ Breanna

Yes, I remember that fight,
        that shirt,
        that room.
I remember your curls
        that summer, when we began
        to realize what we were.
Not random young dreams
        growing in the same light,
        something much more.
I remember when you needed me.
        I remember calling.
        Or how you convinced me
        I was whole
        when I was surely broken.

How can I tell you the ways you help?
How you are the strongest
        half of me, the words I need,
        the laugh on the far side
        of the phone.

We are not disparate dreams
        growing under the same light,
        our long green limbs running
        away from center.
We are ring after ring, the thick and thin,
of our story as we reach
higher and higher
to share the view
I know you deserve.

Grief

5.25.2025

~ Deva

They say grief is love
       with no place to go.
But 'they' haven't been around in a while.
And 'they' never told me that.
So I've been stacking love like many many books
through the hallways of my house.

I've been arranging forests of flowers,
       the colors just so,
       from the eaves, from the gutters,
       pluming like eruptions
       from all the open windows.

I've been cooking your favorite meals
until the table overflows,
       until the dishes run out,
       until even the stairs are a mis en scen
       fit for a Queen, a goddess sacrifice,
       each tread hot and steaming
       with all that I have
       with no place to go.

I cannot navigate the house anymore
so retreat to our spot, the quiet one,
where love need not be stories or acts,
but the ease of the silence we share.

Motorcycle Adventure

9.10.2023
~ Hollis

If I could,
I would bottle it:
      the delicious imbalance
      of acceleration - the raucous bucking
      of the trail that rocks me like a crib.

If I could,
I would keep a flask of it
in the breast pocket
in the desk drawer
the bedside table
buried in the yard out back.

But the hot air, the dramatic vistas,
all the heavy revving,
it never seems to distill down how I need -
despite a perfect recipe.
Critically, 'adventure' permits potential failure.
A difficult ingredient to find - it grows
in the horse-tail streaks of speed unfurling
behind Abandon.

He sits, home and tired, pulls
his flask and drinks deep relishing
the adrenaline, the risk, the youth.

My Dog, My Human

6.28.2023

~ Unknown

You have not always been good. But you have always been loyal.	It feels like endless night without you. But today you are my human.
The mud from last spring will never leave the duvet. And the head of the stick shift - hand polished for years - is forever marred and rough. The price of a momentary chew toy.	You overwhelm but soothe. You confuse, but delight. When you leave, I have nothing With which to remember you until the sound of keys. But you love me in forms I will never understand.
But you understand me and intend so much love. Someday all I will have are these remaining blemishes and the rare dust bunny evicted from the sofa to remember. But today, you are my dog.	You have not always been here but you have always been mine. It's all I could want - more than too much.

In it's original form, this poem appeared the same - with one column of text upside-down - but also had the text on the right in red ink

Chapter Three
Conviction

Anarchist Orca Whales

07.23.2023
~ Luke

You are so funny up there
with your small squirming bodies
always clinging to that side
of heaven.

What do you do with all
that breath -
why are you so desperate
to remain, completely, above?
Your stiff, lifeless vessels
and their deep white veils
extract so much
and return so little.
How could you be so hungry?

We invite you to join our world,
abandon your heady one,
simplify.
We insist.
You make things too complicated,
       too hot, too loud, so empty.
We invite you to slow down,
       hold the breath you have,
       savor it.

Sink and enjoy the silence.
The dark. Let us help you.
You don't even seem to realize
how much you need it.
Hold your breath a while.
Listen.

> *At the time this poem was requested, there was a string of incidents where orca whales were capsizing boats*

Lost in Space: Final Thoughts

7.30.2023

~ Sydney

] The silence has been so long
I am lost in it, speaking
in it: ["" . /// . . "" . . . .]

The black is not so black anymore.
It all ran out
when the thin bowl of the horizon cracked, sank,
became impossible.
I dream in black and shadows: [' __ , -,-'-,-'_,-'-]

My thoughts used to be weightless.
They are my only anchors now.
They are so slow - too fast:
[' . ' . ' . ' . __ __ *-- - - -   -   -   -   ]

Can I be lost if there is only nowhere?
If I am my own planet?
If my final thoughts will echo
in the tomb of me forever?

Can I be lost if I am the only place? [

I remember how a careless moon would catch
in the trees.
And how an effortless emptiness I could not see
would dispel it, free, to the other side.

> *The text in italics was not written as part of*
> *the initial poem, but was added after for social*
> *media. I simply couldn't delete it.*

Fire is a Purifier

8.13.2023

~ Jessica

There is tidy.
Then there is clean.
And then there is the aching empty,
      the purity after
      the world loosens, lightens,
      and turns to smoke.

The soot and ash,
the ugly scar of it, is simple to stare at:
      a nearly two-dimensional frame
      of shades from black to black.

But from this simplicity springs
the next beautiful mess of life.
What is simple is not sterile, not for long.

The trial of the fire condemns it all -
the green, the soft,
all of yesterday. From this simplicity,
the infinite denominator of fire,
springs a tomorrow.

Perhaps the tomorrow we need.
A time that will bloom differently -
feed, inspire, and delight.
A time to carry us further and
one day, to burn.

Fly Fishing

7.30.2024
~ Kevin

Beneath the surface
and its frigid rush
hides, is hiding, hid
and hidden a liquid shadow
flitting between
sight and blindness.

Beneath the surface
of my frustration
hums a steady note -
a focus only the instrument
of the river can play,
a scale only solitude
will know.

> I am not here for the fish.
> I am here for their riddle.
> The melody they overlay
> atop my sinking rhythm.

Beneath the surface
of this rich isolation
I can find what hides,
is hiding, hid, and hidden
in the turbid rush of time.
See what lures will make me rise.
See what color
the depth has made me.

What is the Definition of Happiness

9.27.2023

~ Greta

Of the many doors winking light to dark
in the long corridors of our days,
very few are labeled.
We are, of course, lost
in the branching rooms, the Escher-esque stairs
bringing us from nowhere to nowhere.

But to be lost is not so bad.

We are made to be seeking,
to follow the warm drafts
and their sweet scents as they whisper
through the dark
thresholds of us.

Over time we find the rooms that welcome us
and etch our mark on the door - knowing
we may never find it again.
We linger for a while,
to take in the art on the walls,
but we cannot stay.

After all, we are not made to be finding.
We are to seek.
Can that be our sustenance?
To relish how, not only are we misplaced,
but boldly so.

What To Do With Ones Life

8.25.2024

~ Megan

They say money comes and goes,
but time just goes.

They say 'do what is best'.
Do what is true
and truth is that which does not change.

How am I to be ever going,
never arriving?
      True to a truth
      that cannot grow with me?

They say poetry should not have questions,
that it turns the
world to glass.
They say many things.

They do not answer
the koans I'm asked.
They never said
it's not about the answers,
it's how we romance the mystery.
How we sleep beside the unknown.

How truth comes and goes and
moves and bleeds and
turns me all to glass.

Self Love

8.13.2023
~ Amber

It is flowers.
Not even bloomed.

It is the meal
not yet prepared, but the colors
rumbling along the countertop -
the flavors still asleep.

It is brief:
      just a moment
      and sometimes unexpected,
when our capacity for grace
bursts out, its edges ballooning,
balancing us, buoying us,
and lifting us up.

Love is a practice.
It is the kettle on the stove.
It is the cork on the floor.
It is the letter you wrote,
re-wrote, and never sent.
It is a challenge.
Yet, against all odds,
even when we are cut in half,
we are flowers
who can bloom.

Fate's Arrival

6.25.2023

~ Peter

Perhaps it is easier this way.
To know every false stroke, each misspelling
is/was/will be fate
and therefore, not my fault.

Destiny would be trivial if relegated
to grammar alone.
Rather, it is the decades-old regret,
the words unsaid, the career deferred -
these are the true campaigns in which
we are caught.
The Could- and Should-Have's
Fate swept from the board.

We must not forget the loves,
the inimitable prisms of canopy
that kept us cool on those walks
and keep us young today.
We must not forget Fate's hand in this as well.

But, between you and I,
I prefer to be at the helm -
not spectating some grand shooting match. No,
hand me the dice.
Lay flat for me a blank page that we may see
who is fastest tonight and if I can squeeze
in a typo of my own
before Fate arri_ve

While writing the final line of this poem, the page was caught in the guards and rotated while typing to produce this slanted, incomplete text

Rejection

7.9.2023

~ Alexis

Your cup is large
and could
hold so much of what I have to pour.
      You recoil - you say
      you cannot tolerate the heat,
      how I boil.

Your glass is mesmerizing crystal
shattering light across the walls,
the floor, my face.
      But you cannot stand the
      freezing rush as I let
      what is most precious of me into the light.

I don't need you
to enjoy my hot, my cold,
or to hold me today.
I'd rather pour myself to the ground.
I will refill - I always do.

I'd rather water what will grow
then help you feel full for a moment,
for you to find your leaks and cracks.
I'll not be wasted.
I will be the rain.

Love

7.9.2023
~ Millie

Blast the dams. Flood me.
Let the buoys of my heart
feel their purpose again
for the first time in such a long time.

Of course, after the waters recede,
there is work to do. The muddy trails
are tangled and so many
who came before were lost.
We do our best.
And our best requires bravery.

That of us which is to be loved
cannot be found on the paved roads or beaten paths.
That of us which is to be loved
will not be found behind us.
We must abandon the trails, reject
their safety, and lose the light in the forest.
Follow something else,
choose our own north,
and find our ocean in which to swim.

Love

10.1.2023
~ Rachel

For something that assumes
so much space within us,
love imparts such a mild flavor.
When it speaks or sings,
it is distant, almost too faint to find.
It dances slow and in the shadows,
and when it finally blooms, the scent
       is loose and underwhelming.

It's easy to believe, at times,
love is dormant or simply gone.
This is dangerous - when we consider
it has left. When we think it foolish
       to leave dinner outside its door.

We are human and are thus allowed our errors.
That love dares to live within us
at all is a blessing:
       we are unreliable hosts.

But we are so dependent. We offer up
all our rooms, search a week
for a trace of you.
Stop quickly in the hallway
when we feel the warmth
of where you must have been. We inhale,
smell just enough & smile.

Baby Daddy aka Cheating Ass

9.24.2022

~ Anonymous

I can almost remember
those good qualities
I thought you had.

I can almost remember
why you seemed like a fine
investment for this Kashmir
heart which I ripped
on the cut corners, sharp eyes,
and rough edges that you are.

I can almost remember how I wanted to see you.
Almost.
Instead, I'll remember the heat
of burning your cabinet of memories
I had kept so clean and safe in my head.

I almost lit your cash on fire,
but instead, I'll crumple it into a poem
so I can remember
why you were worth burning.

The woman who requested this prompt donated using money given to her by her (ex)boyfriend

Healing

5.9.2025

~ Kassidy

Implies a breaking
which in turn implies
a wholeness
which may, when used improperly,
imply completion.
As if the algebra of our hearts
      adopted an X here
      and a () there
      to reach the perfect
      cleanliness of 0.
           Clean but static.
           Perhaps whole,
           but empty.

We must remember:
we were whole before it all started -
not some theory of zero.
We were messy, confusing,
      line after line of arithmetic
      down and off the page.
      We were joy
      and frustration and bewilderment at ourselves.

Simplify. Begin with one
and start counting. You'll find
yourself soon enough.
Count the clouds, the leaves,
the grass - all the ways
you can love yourself.

New Beginnings

Date Unknown

~ Anonymous

No one can make you feel the change underfoot
as the path you were on
becomes a path with no destination.

The bends and climbs are different then. The rivers
you parallel run deeper, colder.
The silence between the dark trunks
swallows more of you -
sometimes all of you.

The fires you nurture
will still feel like home,
but only the windows in which you can look.
That is all you need of home today.
No one will feel it for you:
        how the new trail reaches up
        to kiss the bottoms of your feet,
        how the mute of the forest cracks you open
        or how, when so far from everything,
        the roof reaches ridgeline to ridgeline.

Chapter Four

Hope

Change

7.9.2023

~ Erin

We are not who we were yesterday.
Thank God.
I liked them fine enough.
They meant well and knew
how to have a good time.
But sometimes
it felt as though
they kept their world so small.
With so much potential - a bigger love,
      a work that gathers me up
      in the crucible of intent
      and shoves me off the edge.

Such a relief
when we learn we do not have to be
who we have been.
It's exhausting to stay so static.
To shrug off
what holds us in place
allows us room to dance
the way we always wanted.

We are not who we were yesterday.
Thank God.
Tomorrow is calling
and I already have some revisions -
though I'll be keeping the good times.

New Beginnings

Date Unknown

~ Anonymous

The best are accidents.
When it's not a new destination
that pulls you from your path,
but a wrong turn.
Maybe poor direction.
A brief lapse of focus
as you wander beneath the thick shade
of what was your typical route
the old you would take.

You picked up and could not replace
a perfectly broken compass.
Pointing you to a perfect accident,
a perfect misstep,
        a fortuitous stumble
        into a chapter not listed
        in the index
        where the pages are not numbered,
        the characters with new names,
        and the plot thickens.

Put your old novel down.
Flip through a new title.
Write your own ending.

Welcome to Your Twenties

5.19.2024

~ Zaza

It's important to stress:
       they are yours
       and no one else's.
They are yours to bend & break
and mend & mark;
       to revisit & cherish,
       waste & forget.
You will wear them like
face paint, like bruises,
       like feathers, like clouds
       on strings tied to your
       dreams and a whole sky
           of tomorrow rushing
                to be filled.

You will learn what you like -
small gifts all of them
like seeds in the duff
forgotten by the sun,
some the dark mystery of who
you can become:
       some storm, some animus
       in the not-so-fragile buds that yearn
       to burst up and down
       the rough edges of you.

We would give advice,
but the greatest gift is looking back
to see the purity of one's mistakes -
the garden before
it ruptured to beauty.

Sunday at the Farmers Market

10.1.2023
~ Shelby

On the 7th day, we rest.
Not the commandment we expect these days.
When the rush towards the budget,
      the bottom line,
      the next meeting
      can be all-consuming.
We are almost adapted to constant motion,
ceaseless production,
and plastic,
      packaged,
            pervasive entertainment
            to fill the gaps.
Almost adapted.

When the body slows enough
for the heart to quiet,
the echoes to settle, we are
sometimes startled
by who we are left with.

Once again in conversation
with just ourselves, we see
the pieces we forgot -
      the tender parts, the shy ones
      that obey our most vital tenets:
      the ones that make us human -
      and yet more so.

Our memories of the fresh-cut grass,
the first exhale of summer, the breadcrumbs
of who we were and who we may be.

Embarking on a New Chapter

9.17.2023

~ Kelsey

We water diligently
and weed with fervor.
All the while watching
       our harvest dress itself -
       a performance from which we can
       hardly look away.

We learn many things
and the season treats us well.
When we taste, however,
we see that we were not wrong
so much as what we needed then
we do not hunger for now.

It is not a betrayal.
It is not a loss.
It is seeds for which we are no longer fertile.
It is pointless to plant them.

Of course, we have only tasted
the rustic palette of our past.
The recipes we know by heart.

It is not a betrayal.
It is not a loss
to search for distant fields.
The heart wants what the heart wants.
Our job is to feed it the best we can -
no matter how far the field.

Nervous to Talk to New People

8.13.2023

~ Skye

He says, (.. .. .. ..)
and I wonder what he's forming in his head.
I know I'm not too scary -
few poets are.
I know I saw him whispering.
And I think I may just know
what (.. .. .. ..) really means.

It's not the people outside
that concern us quite folk. No,
it's how precious our gentle thoughts are within -
vibrant humming dreams which have not seen
the light just yet.
Have not had to walk on their own two feet
beyond the limits of one's skull.
What if they stumble?
What if they fall?

I won't tell you it isn't scary.
But I will promise you:
it's when we let our thoughts take wing
that we are most free -
when we watch them run,
hop and soar away, their shadows
wheeling in the light.

First Love

5.25.2025
~ Cadence

The poet sighs and begins
to count his loves. It is a number
greater than one.

The poet sighs and resolves to NOT do
what poets are SUPPOSED to do:
    tell you what something
    is.
        How something
                feels.

A first love is much too precious to handle,
even with gloves, out on the street.

No, it is not to be sketched
    or dressed or named
    by anyone but you.
Only you get to say:
    this is how I feel.
Only you get to wrap this in ribbons
    or hide it in the garden;
    only you get to throw it from the roof
    or braid it in your hair.

Only you are to limit how free, how big,
    how light, or how seen
    your love can make you.

Do this poet a favor: go write it down.
    Show us what poetry can be.

Heartbreak

6.25.2023

~ Tess

This will not soothe you today.
And tomorrow may be lost as well.
But there will be a morning
      when this truth
      helps swing your feet over the edge
      and set them to the ground
      with a new levity.

Truth is light and easy to carry
and so you should know:
      Hearts are designed for breaking.
      The hidden creases and trap doors
      collapse so seamlessly,
      can leave no tracks or traces,
      a magic trick so perfect
            the destruction feels permanent.

Hearts are designed to fold flat
and to be lost amidst old receipts
and takeout menus.
Truth is light and easy to carry.
So fold this paper flat and lose it
in your purse a while.
You will find it soon -
just as you will find your heart
perhaps some morning waiting
in your coffee mug
whole, happy, and magic.

Phoenix

6.9.2024
~ Quinn

We all know the flames
and discuss the ash at length.
The rebirth.
The impossibly elegant circuit
      of destruction
           & its unblemished
                reanimation.

We can assume the heat, the pain -
perhaps even the sense
of a refreshed perspective.

But we cannot imagine
      the confusion:
      blinking open into a smoky light,
      the lingering scent of who we were,
      the grey remains
      of what we left behind
      and, presumably, no longer need.

Confusion is a good place to start I suppose.
A fine way to begin our search, to explore
this landscape we once knew.
To plant in us the unavoidable dream,
the impossible need to fly.

Water

6.25.2023
~ Daren

We search for you in the cold
bowels of distant planets.

We dam you and bottle you.
We rash you with fishing nets,
refuse, and plastic bags.

I promise, we are trying.
Trying to learn all the lessons
you teach. We are not yet
fluid, still and fast -
we are not yet flowing downhill
to clean and feed.

But we are trying.
We are getting better
at holding each other close,
uniting like beads of rain.
We practice freezing or lifting off
to be what our temperature needs of us.

We are unearthing the deep pipes
where we run our emotions
and instead let them course
in open words, open air.

We search for you like we search
for the best in us.
We need you like we need love -
falling from the sky.

Mushrooms & Seasonal Depressnnnnnnnn

5.5.2024

~ Will

The damn sun has been scared of me all winter.
Cold and distant, clouded
and wrapped in riddles, it spools
from my head:
      the thin strand from my ear
      like a kite string
      up into nothing.
           When I give a tug
           nothing resists,
           nothing responds.

The damn sun pretends to be weightless,
pretends I don't need it.

But many things have moved beyond
their first love,
their first addiction.
The first year, when the dark
swallowed so much of them.

Mushrooms grow even in the dark. In the storm.
In my floating head
and its wet wrap of taught thread
squeezing so tight the rain runs out
and the mushrooms thank me,
ask me if I'd like to hear a song.

Saturn 29

6.9.2024

~ Paige

Well, that was fun while it lasted - those plans
    I had for me; that progress I made.
    The me I thought I was.
Far away - further than I can fit in my head -
    the clock of my soul is chiming.

The great ringing of our flaming bell
sends the citizen of my heart scattering:
    students leave their chairs,
    bankers close the tellers,
    a lover leaves the bed
        to catch the last train
and I *or who I was*
is standing in the middle of the hot street
holding a bag of something I no longer need
missing someone I can't remember,
    unsure how I feel
as the gentle song of the universe
sends a new shiver
through my nerves,
spins the dial of north and south -
sends me on my way.

An astrological concept, 'Saturn 29' refers
to one full circuit of Saturn and in turn,
represents a shfit in one's identity and purpose

Florida.Hot.Queer.Welcome

8.13.2023
~ Leah

The weather is uninviting for some:
the cotton ball heat gathering
between skin & shirt, skin & sun,
skin and the hard eyes
of those who seem so comfortable here.

We make it work: we adapt and we adjust.
We change our clothes to feel ok.
We talk about the weather,
though some deem it boring, pedestrian,
just hot air.

But what could be more important
the rising tides, the stifling rooms,
the heat mounting higher, higher
higher.

We make it work. It's not always easy.
We tolerated the cotton ball heat
and changing our styles.
We will not change more:
we cannot change our skin.
The weather is best
felt bare anyway.

Love

9.10.2023
~ Henry

So much work for one word -
        to hold us all together.
        To bring forth the light
        of our sometimes-tired world.

Love, (n): the sweet silence
        when the laundry - still warm
        lies forgotten
        on the bed. We are delinquent
        & laughing in the other room.

Love, (v): singing the song
        you've carried since childhood,
        windows down, until
        you stop tearing up.
        Until my voice is silly & hoarse.

Lovely, (adj): the sleeping cat,
        steam rising from my mug:
        an evening I will surely forget -
        its deliciousness fading
        before the tea even cools.

How we sign our letters, how we hold hands,
how we birth our art,
how&how&how
but also - and necessarily - why.

Cheese

11.5.2024
~ Katie

Crumble. Cream.
      Flakes.
      An array of
      phenotypes
      hidden behind the rind.

After we set you in the dark
and permit you the time
to become hard or soft,
rough or smooth,
we all wait for the reveal.

Some alchemy in the blackness
we covet, that we want
for ourselves.
As if the right meditation
underground could coax forth
the correct maturity
of our spirit -
could relieve us of our liquid
dissatisfaction.

Endured silence does not answer
our questions.

This joy is not learned,
it is felt.
Tasted even.

To Coach

2.10.2024

~ Anonymous

We came to you with plenty
of energy and Olympic focus -
      you'd surely agree we never
      get distracted ...
And that was all you needed
to teach us gravity, show us speed,
and explain the nuance of balance.

But that is not the only task
a coach must perform.
There are lessons
between the lessons:
      balance is more than the body in poise,
      it is the patience you gave us.
      To vault takes more than strength alone,
      it needs the focus to which you brought us.
      And to walk out alone on the floor
      is more than posture,
      it is a confidence
      to which you guided us.

We came to you with much,
but are leaving with so much more.
Thank you for the lessons
you wrapped in jokes.
Answers wrapped in balance.

This poem was requested by a young girl as a gift to her gymnastics coach

Summer to Fall

9.10.2023
~ Stephanie

It is not always apparent
when we first begin to change colors -
our summer drifting inevitably, impossibly,
to fall.

A gentle fatigue of comfort.
The soft oxbows draining
from us as we cool.

Hope is ripe and we will harvest.
Our fields of desire are rich,
but fallow. And then there is
the upper pasture
where we don't mend the fences,
where the stock is not so domesticated,
and where the first of the orange and reds
bloom in the back of our hearts.
It will be some time before we can see the change
from the porch, before the frost
prompts our fires.

So today, I trek up to the pasture
and call for them -
call to see if they recognize me;
to see if I am who I was or if, overnight,
I became the mystery of tomorrow.
Red and blooming.

Resiliency

8.20.2023
~ Gretchen

We do not ask for invincibility.
We do not ask for eternity.
This humility grants us
other gifts -
      the silly intimacy
      we share with the dawn;
      the glance imparting 1,000 words
      before they look away.
      Those moments
      when we are light and clean
      and mortal. When we feel it.

No, we ask for strength.
      For regrowth. For progress.
      We go to the fields,
      to the silly sunrise,
      to the great poets
      for that sustenance.

We do not ask for the gods
to plant something within us.
We seek the polished instants
when the world reminds us
what we already have deep down.
It is work to dredge it up into the light.
It is hard, silly work.

So here is a reminder of that deep down.
An echo? The shadow leaking light at dawn?
Not the sunrise, not yet.
But the promise of it.

A Tortoise Shell Cat Named: Rude

7.9.2023
~ Nikki

We never know what we agree to
when we let them in our house.
Especially a cat.
The truth is, they obey nothing
regardless of pacts, treaties,
or ceasefires.
No, they are unfettered -
      no sit, no stay,
      no commands.
Rather, we are subject to the
fay affections and in

                            con

            sist

                            encies

of temperament.

The binding resolution we forge
when they first cross our threshold
is between ourselves
and who we want to be.
The cat is, of course, uninvolved
in the way we expect.

After years of negotiations
they never cede.
Yet somehow, against our wishes,
they make us precisely who we need to be.

A Squid Who is in Love with the Sun

7.30.2023
~ Sydney

Somehow you are warmth -
a body I can feel, but cannot
touch.

I draw you mandalas in the sand,
watch your refracted laughter
wrinkle and scatter - silent
beneath the surface.

I ask the whales with their beautiful
voices to sing my song
or even just a message.
They tell me you do not respond.

But usually, before you go,
you dash yourself gold and red
onto the waves and I think,
this is love.

In this fair ocean where we lay our scene,
the walls are much too high to climb - the top
where you wander, is too alien
and hurts too much.
We will never be together.
Somehow you are warmth, a body
I can feel, but cannot touch.
Somehow, my love, that is enough.

The world needs more poetry.

To contact, email: adbpoetry@gmail.com
To donate, Venmo: @adb_poetry
To read, Instagram: @adb_poetry

www.ingramcontent.com/pod-product-compliance
Lightning Source LLC
Chambersburg PA
CBHW031420160426
43196CB00008B/1003